**REBUILDING
PUBLIC
INSTITUTIONS
TOGETHER**

T0324383

McCourtney Institute for Democracy

The Pennsylvania State University's McCourtney Institute for Democracy (democracyinstitute.la.psu.edu) was founded in 2012 as an interdisciplinary center for research, teaching, and outreach on democracy. The institute coordinates innovative programs and projects in collaboration with the Center for American Political Responsiveness and the Center for Democratic Deliberation.

Laurence and Lynne Brown Democracy Medal

The Laurence and Lynne Brown Democracy Medal recognizes outstanding individuals, groups, and organizations that produce exceptional innovations to further democracy in the United States or around the world. In even numbered years, the medal spotlights practical innovations, such as new institutions, laws, technologies, or movements that advance the cause of democracy. Awards given in odd numbered years highlight advances in democratic theory that enrich philosophical conceptions of democracy or empirical models of democratic behavior, institutions, or systems.

REBUILDING PUBLIC INSTITUTIONS TOGETHER

PROFESSIONALS AND CITIZENS IN A PARTICIPATORY DEMOCRACY

ALBERT W. DZUR

CORNELL SELECTS
An imprint of
CORNELL UNIVERSITY PRESS
Ithaca and London

Cornell Selects, *an imprint of Cornell University Press, provides a forum for advancing provocative ideas and fresh viewpoints through outstanding digital and print publications. Longer than an article and shorter than a book, titles published under this imprint explore a diverse range of topics in a clear and concise format—one designed to appeal to any reader. Cornell Selects publications continue the Press's long tradition of supporting high quality scholarship and sharing it with the wider community, promoting a culture of broad inquiry that is a vital aspect of the mission of Cornell University.*

First published 2018 by Cornell University Press

Printed in the United States of America

Library of Congress Cataloging-in-Publication Data

Names: Dzur, Albert W., author.
Title: Rebuilding public institutions together : professionals and citizens
   in a participatory democracy / Albert W. Dzur.
Description: Ithaca : Cornell Selects, an imprint of Cornell University
   Press, 2018. | Includes bibliographical references and index.
Identifiers: LCCN 2017038569 (print) | LCCN 2017041288 (ebook) |
   ISBN 9781501721991 (epub/mobi) | ISBN 9781501722004 (pdf) |
   ISBN 9781501721984 | ISBN 9781501721984 (pbk.: alk. paper)
Subjects: LCSH: Social advocacy—United States. | Professional employees—
   Political activity—United States. | Professional ethics—United States. |
   Political participation—Moral and ethical aspects—United States. |
Classification: LCC HV95 (ebook) | LCC HV95 .D983 2018 (print) |
   DDC 361.60973—dc23
LC record available at https://lccn.loc.gov/2017038569

Cornell University Press strives to use environmentally responsible suppliers and materials to the fullest extent possible in the publishing of its books. Such materials include vegetable-based, low-VOC inks and acid-free papers that are recycled, totally chlorine-free, or partly composed of nonwood fibers. For further information, visit our website at cornellpress.cornell.edu.

Work as if you live in the early days of a better nation.

—Alasdair Gray

Contents

**REBUILDING
PUBLIC
INSTITUTIONS
TOGETHER**

Introduction

I want us to get a better grip on democracy, as a concept, because we often set either too low or too high a standard. In some high school and college government textbooks, democracy is achieved merely by following the rules, obeying the law, and showing up to vote (when we feel strongly enough, that is). In other, more philosophical conversations, democracy is attained only when certain cognitive, deliberative, or distributive demands are met that protect decision-making forums from public ignorance, strategic bargaining, and resource inequalities. By contrast, I want to bring things down to earth: to specific places, routines, and above all, to specific people in proximity to one another sharing tasks, information, and decisions. Democracy means sharing power to shape a common public life with others who are not the same as us. This is more demanding than rule-following, obedience, and voting, but it also differs from the philosophers' standards.

Consent, legitimacy, sovereignty, and myriad other terms used in political theory can sound legalistic and formal, as if democracy were only about laws, regulations, and voting rules. Instead of the legal, regulative, and electoral, however, I want to stress the productive as being the vital core of democracy: we share tasks that constitute us as a people—we produce education, justice, security, and more.[1] We learn how to do this task-sharing activity well or poorly, consciously or not, in schools, workplaces, street corners, hospitals, courtrooms, and many other places. Cognition does not drive democratic work in such places; it follows it. Laws and rules help shape institutions that allow citizens to act, of course, but it is the action itself that makes them democratic.

Pessimism pervades contemporary thinking about democracy. In academia, some worry about "oligarchic" and "neoliberal" power while others raise alarms about "populist" and "demotic" influence. Outside the university, widespread distrust of politics and politicians is common, as is a pervasive lack of trust in each other as resources for long-term constructive social change.

I think this pessimism and distrust is deeply rooted in the nonparticipatory and professionally managed public world Americans live in. Yes, we have social movements, but many civil society groups have become top-down hierarchical organizations that mobilize support, fundraise, and advocate narrowly for an otherwise unlinked membership population.[2] Where once such groups tutored people in the practical communication, interpersonal, and organizational skills useful for effective civic participation, today they are managed by increasingly professionalized staff. Yes we have politics, but in government too, public institutions that could welcome, indeed require, citizen contributions simply do not. Courts, for example, once heard most cases through a jury trial made up of citizens acting—for a few days—as part of their government. Now only 1 to 4 percent of state and federal criminal cases reach the trial stage, with the rest plea bargained or settled.[3]

We might suspect, and we wouldn't be wrong, that the organization of modern life is unfriendly to democracy. We have good reason to be anxious about concentrations of power and nontransparency in our institutions. If we know where to look, however, we will see some powerful examples of democratic innovation that could point a way out of our current situation. Collective work in unassuming, everyday places is happening all around us and inviting us in.

I

This Problem Belongs to Everyone

L et's start at Forest Grove Community School, located in a coastal agricultural community about an hour's drive from Portland, Oregon. During recess one spring day, some seventh-grade students are playing basketball. Classroom tensions spill over into the game. Two boys closely guard another boy and steal the ball from him, repeatedly. He gets mad and lashes out, hitting one of the opponents.

When the victim's father is notified that his son was hit, he immediately asks the principal to suspend the offender, or else he will call the police and charge the boy with assault. The principal, Vanessa Gray, has a different idea. She begins by meeting with a group of students who were on the playground at the time of the incident to talk about what happened. Then she brings all three of the basketball players into her office one by one. The bystanders and the main actors all confirm that the facts of the case are not in dispute. Principal Gray allows the victim to go home, sends his teammate back to class, and keeps the perpetrator in her office for a while to talk. Before sending him home for the day, she tells him that there are going to be some further conversations when he comes back to school.

The next day the conferencing begins, and Principal Gray tells the three students they can't play basketball until they have a congress with all the basketball players about what the rules are going to be as they go forward with the game. She later relates, in a series of interviews I conducted with innovators in a number of professional fields, "I really wanted these three to understand: they messed up the basketball game. And I wanted the other basketball players to understand that they were bystanders. They knew that these tensions were going on a long time before it erupted and before I knew about it. I wanted them to understand they had a responsibility to right a wrong and there are lots of ways for them to do it."

Gray encourages all the students to use their voice. She comes to understand that the perpetrator needs to develop his communication skills for times when he feels stressed and frustrated. In her one-on-one conversation with him, she explains, "You always have a voice. You don't have to hit somebody to make a point. Your voice can get loud; sometimes that's appropriate to say, 'Back OFF!!' really loudly. That gets the point across."

In addition, Principal Gray takes responsibility for her own role in the conflict, acknowledging to the perpetrator that he had come to her earlier in the year to say that sometimes, basketball was tense:

> This is really helpful for me to try to do a better job of trying to understand what a kid is communicating to me; and you, kid, you need to learn a little more about how to use your voice. The way you expressed the tensions on the basketball court was in the same tone you use when you tell me that school is boring or you're going skiing this weekend. What you said did not make me concerned that you were angry. And I'm wondering if your way of expressing your frustration with your classmates has also been similarly flat and that you need to work on feeling more comfortable with saying, "Hey, I'm upset!" "I'm mad!" "I want someone to do something about it!" "I want someone to work with me on this."

What does this story tell us about democracy? It tells us what one person can do to shape an institutional environment that welcomes rather than discourages deliberation and collective action. Rather than sealing off a problem, attributing blame to a specific central actor, and taking ownership of it as simple disciplinary matter for the administration or police to take care of, Principal Gray does four things: she makes the problem public; she has conversations with everyone involved; she spreads out responsibility for the conflict and includes herself; and she empowers everyone involved—including bystanders and others in the school—to figure out ways of creating more peaceful basketball games at recess. Yes, the violence should not have happened, and yes, there was a perpetrator and a victim. But the participatory process Gray uses focuses on the interactions that caused the tension, and that focus allows her to help students themselves play a bigger role in solving the problem by developing the skills they need to have better games, classroom discussions, and other collective projects in the future.

Vanessa Gray's school is a field of democratic agency where hierarchical relationships—in this case between adults and kids—are relaxed, and where shared responsibility for core problems—in this case, social order—is encouraged. Is it easy to do this? No. Is it time-consuming? Yes. But I don't see how we grow an active and alert democratic culture without institutions like this helping to build up our capability for social ordering and other public tasks.

This story also teaches us that participatory democracy is no utopian dream, but rather a lot of small, imperfect, fluid, sometimes time-consuming efforts. True, Forest Grove is one small part of a big country, so it might be utopian to think participatory innovations can spread, grow, and sustain themselves as an ongoing culture. We will return to this question, but for now let us note that the people at Forest Grove Community School are choosing to work together on common problems. They are not dreaming; they are doing. They are acting to close the social distances between each student and between the students and an institution that looms so large in young lives.

II

What Is a Democratic Professional?

Vanessa Gray is a democratic professional. Innovators like her are working in education, journalism, criminal justice, health care, city government, and other fields today. They are democratic professionals not because they do democracy really professionally, but because they do professionalism really democratically. They are democratizing specific parts of our public world that have become professionalized: our schools, newspapers, TV stations, police departments, courts, probation offices, prisons, hospitals, clinics, government agencies, among others. They use their professional training, capabilities, and authority to help people—in Vanessa Gray's case, students—in their fields of action to solve problems together, and even more important, to recognize the kinds of problems they need to solve.

They share previously professionalized tasks and encourage lay participation in ways that enhance and enable collective action and deliberation about major social issues inside and outside professional domains.

Professionalism, broadly understood, has important meanings and implications for individuals, groups, and society at large. To be a professional is to have a commitment to competence in a specific field of action—you pursue specialized skills and knowledge so you can act well in difficult situations. Professionals understand their work as having an important normative core: beyond simply earning a living, the work serves society somehow. Sociologists of the professions stress the ways occupations draw boundaries around certain tasks, claim special abilities to handle them, police the ways in which they are discharged, and monitor education and training. Democratic professionalism is an alternative to a conventional model of professionalism I call *social trustee professionalism*, yet it is also different from some other approaches critical of professional power, which I call the *radical critique*.

The social trustee ideal emerged in the 1860s and held prominence for a century among traditional professions such as law and medicine as well as aspiring professions such as engineering and social work. It holds that professionals have a more general responsibility than just a fiduciary or function-specific obligation to their clients.[4] Of course, professionals are obligated to competently perform their tasks, but they also have general responsibilities that stem from their social status, the trust clients place in them, and the market protection governments have permitted them through licensing and other regulations. As Talcott Parsons put it, "A full-fledged profession must have some institutional means of making sure . . . competence will be put to socially responsible uses."[5] For example, the medical profession heals people, but it also contributes to the larger social goals of curing disease and improving public health. And the legal profession, besides defending their clients' rights, also upholds the social conception of justice.

Social trustee professionals may represent public interests in principle, but in fact this representation is very abstract. Serving "the community" is not seen by professionals as something that requires much say from diverse members of actual, present-day communities. Under the terms of the social trustee model, professionals serve the public through their commitment to high standards of practice, a normative orientation toward a sphere of social concern—doctors and health, lawyers and justice—and self-regulation. The model is held together on the basis of an economy of trust: the public trusts the professionals to self-regulate and determine standards of practice, while the professionals earn that trust by performing competently and adhering to the socially responsible normative orientation. Those public administrators, for example, who see themselves as social trustees assert quite straightforwardly that they are hired to manage issues for which they have specialized training—public budgeting, town planning, and the orchestration of service provision, among others. If their communities disapprove of the way they do their jobs, they can fire them, but true professionals do not need to listen to their communities.

A radical critique emerged in the 1960s, drawing attention to the ways professions can be impediments to the democratic expression of public interests rather than trustworthy representatives. Though aware of the benefits of modern divisions of labor that distribute tasks to different groups of people with specialized training for the sake of efficiency, productivity, and innovation, critics like Ivan Illich and Michel Foucault worried about task monopolies secured by professionals that block participation, shrink the space of democratic authority, and disable and immobilize citizens who might occupy that space.[6]

Professions shrink the space of democratic authority when they perform public purposes that could conceivably be done by laypeople—as doctors aid human welfare and criminal justice administrators serve needs for social order. Critics stressed that these services and products have public consequences: how they are done affects people not just as individuals but also as members of an ongoing collective. And sometimes professionals quite literally shrink the space of participation by deciding public issues in institutions, far from potential sites of citizen awareness and action. Think of how health care professionals promote certain kinds of treatment and healing over others and how criminal justice professionals construct complex anger management and life-skills programming for convicted offenders. Professionals can disable and immobilize because, in addition to taking over these tasks, their sophistication in, say, healing or sentencing makes people less comfortable with relying on their own devices for wellness and social order. Professions are professions by virtue of their utilization of abstract, specialized, or otherwise esoteric knowledge to serve social needs such as health or justice. The status and authority of professional work depend on the deference of nonmembers—their acknowledgment that professionals perform these tasks better than untrained others. But with deference comes the risk that members of the general public lose confidence in their own competence—not only where the task itself is concerned, but for making informed collective decisions about issues that relate to professional domains of action.

How can professional actors help mobilize rather than immobilize, expand rather than shrink democratic authority? The radical critique leaves this question largely unexplored. Critics offer few alternatives to social trusteeism for reform-minded practitioners who wish to be both professional and democratic: to deprofessionalize or to develop highly self-reflective and acutely power-sensitive forms of professional practice that draw attention to the ways traditional practices and institutions block and manipulate citizens. Yet these reform suggestions fail to register the ways professional power can be constructive for democracy. To

Table 1: Models of professionalism

	Social trustee	Radical critique	Democratic professionalism
Main characteristics of a profession	Knowledge, self-regulation, social responsibility	Power to define interests for the public	Commitment to knowledge, but also to codirection of professional services
Source of professionals' social duties	Group experience, functional purposes, tacit exchange	Interest in retaining status and market security	Professional training and experience, but also from public collaboration
Professionals' view of laypeople	Clients, consumers, wards	Incompetent at high-level tasks	Citizens with a stake in professional decisions
Professionals' ideal role in society	Expert, specialist, guide	Deprofessionalize, resist temptation to monopolize tasks	Share authority and knowledge through task-sharing
Political role of professions	Protect professional interests and social functions	Disabling intermediary between citizens and institutions	Enabling intermediary between citizens and institutions

the extent that professionals serve as barriers and disablers, they can also, if motivated, serve as barrier removers and enablers. Especially in complex, fast-paced modern societies, professional skills and knowledge help laypeople manage personal and collective affairs. What we need is not an antiprofessionalism, but a democratic professionalism oriented toward public capability.

So, how might democratic professionals go about their work? While heeding the conventional obligation to serve social purposes, they also seek to avoid perpetuating the civic disenfranchisement noticed by radical critics of professional power. Democratic professionals relate to society in a particular way: rather than using their skills and expertise as they see fit for the good of others, they aim to understand the world of the patient, the offender, the client, the student, and the citizen on their terms—and then work collaboratively on common problems. They regard the layperson's knowledge and agency as critical components in resolving what can all-too-easily be seen as strictly professional issues: education, government, health, justice, and more.

Two Paths of Democratic Change

Democratic professionals in the United States and elsewhere are already creating power-sharing arrangements in institutions that are usually hierarchical and nonparticipatory. They can help us understand the resources available right now for deep cultural change. To appreciate this, however, we must release ourselves from the grip of the prevailing view of how and where democratic change happens.

Drawing on the historical precedents of abolition, women's suffrage, labor reform, civil rights, and student movements, discussion of democratic change typically focuses on the power of people joined together in common cause to press for major legislative action. Core factors in the process include leadership, mobilization, organizational capacity, consciousness-raising, forms of protest such as strikes, marches, and sit-ins, and electoral pressure on political parties and candidates.

While our default perspective is crucial for understanding some types of democratic action, it is state-centric and privileges resources that are *exogenous* to daily life. In this first path to democratic change, political action appears as a burst of collective energy that then dissipates after certain legal or policy targets are met: slavery abolished, voting rights for women established, the eight-hour workday guaranteed, military conscription for Vietnam ended. A large-enough number of people temporarily leave their everyday routines to join a collective effort. For this reason, some scholars call democratic movements "fugitive," since at the end of the protest or campaign, most people return home, leaving the business of government to insiders.[7]

Less noticed are the alterations democratic professionals make to their institutions as they break down internal hierarchies and foster physical proximity between people, encourage coownership of problems previously seen as too complex for laypeople, and seek out opportunities for collaborative work. We fail to see these activities as politically significant because they do not fit our conventional picture of democratic change.

The reformers I have interviewed in my ongoing research on democratic professionals in criminal justice, public administration, education, and other fields rarely use social science or political theory concepts. Lacking ideology, they make it up as they go along, developing roles, attitudes, habits, and practices that open up rigid structures to greater participation. In this second path to democratic change, democratic action is *endogenous* to an occupational routine, often involving those who would not consider themselves activists—or even engaged citizens. Though they often belong to practitioner networks, the innovators I have met do not form a typical social movement. Rather than mobilizing fellow activists and putting pressure on government officeholders to make new laws or rules, democratic professionals make changes in their domains themselves, piece by piece, practice by practice. In the trenches all around us, they are renovating and reconstructing schools, clinics, prisons, and other seemingly inert bodies.

In State College, Pennsylvania, principal Donnan Stoicovy turned her kindergarten-through-fifth-grade school

Table 2: Two paths of democratic change

	Social movements	**Democratic professionals**
Driving force	Cognitive shifts	Proximity
Sites	Outside formal bodies	Inside formal bodies
Goals	Law or policy change	Role, habit, practice change
Participation	Optional	Not fully voluntary

into an explicitly "democratic" school by designing curricula and internal structures to encourage student voice and participation. Restorative justice practitioner Lauren Abramson has held community justice conferences in some of the most distressed neighborhoods in Baltimore, Maryland, so that citizens themselves could address harmful actions before they enter the criminal justice system. City manager Kimball Payne mitigated racial tensions in Lynchburg, Virginia, through citizen engagement embedded in city government. These and many other democratic professionals are changing everyday practices where people live and work. The democratic action they help make possible is therefore not "fugitive" because it is part of the routines of daily life.

Democratic professionals have leverage on the social world, but it differs from that of the political actors and movement organizers we are used to. The energy involved is not a large burst, but a slow burn fueled not by a shift in public consciousness, but through load-bearing work that fosters relations of proximity within classrooms, conference rooms, and administrative offices, all of them spaces newly reopened to the public as civic spaces.[8] This proximity in public space—getting close enough to see and understand others as fellow citizens—is taken for granted, and yet it is in astonishingly short supply. We live in a democracy, but it is very easy to go through life without ever working democratically on a public problem with others who differ from oneself in terms of race, class, or education.

Asocial Structures and the Proximity Deficit

Indeed, even in the first half of the nineteenth century, astute observers noticed that alongside highly participatory elements of American democracy, such as frequent elections, town meetings, and jury trials, significant evasions of civic responsibility and cultivated lack of political awareness were also present. Alexis de Tocqueville saw what he called "individualism" as a common vice of the new world; not the selfishness or egoism he was accustomed to in Europe, but a cool conscious retreat from the public sphere into the familial private domain. Americans could go off into the forests of Michigan, build cabins, farm, hunt, and live quietly without contributing much to the outside world or relying on it.[9] Tocqueville saw this as a personal, if ultimately mistaken, choice made possible by relative equality of conditions and bountiful natural resources.

John Dewey, writing a hundred years later in his 1927 book, *The Public and Its Problems*, worried similarly about the difficulties individuals had in joining up in collective action. For Dewey, though, it was the complexity of the public world and not the inducements of the private life that constituted the main problem. The modern public, he wrote, was in eclipse, too "scattered, mobile, and manifold" to find itself. To be sure, twentieth-century Americans inherited a participatory infrastructure—town meetings, local control, competitive elections—but it was inadequate for an era of urban populations, large-scale corporations, and cross-regional issues. Democracy, Dewey thought, "consists in having a responsible share according to capacity in forming and directing the activities of the groups to which one belongs and in participating according to need in the values which the groups sustain."[10] But how could individuals awaken to this responsibility and adequately discharge it under conditions that bewilder them and obscure common interests?

Now, ninety years later, the public is even more scattered, mobile, and manifold. Public squares, parks, and other places of unexpected meetings and common experiences are often displaced by commercialized private spaces. Sociologists write of contemporary social structures that, paradoxically, destructure common life, distance us from one another, and make it increasingly hard for us to interact in anything but a partial, superficial, and self-selecting fashion. Zygmunt Bauman coins a term, *adiaphorization*, for how modern society exerts a "soporific influence" that prevents "individuals from awakening to their 'mutual dependencies' and so to their mutual responsibilities."[11] This helps update Tocqueville's and Dewey's analyses: individualism under modern conditions of adiaphorization is not merely a matter of choosing to retreat from the complicated, unattractive public world to a more attractive private life; it is, rather, a social aspect of a public world that has itself become narrowly segmented:

> It is not that the solidary life is in trouble because of the inborn self-interest of "inadequately socialized" individuals. The opposite is the case: individuals tend to be self-centered and self-engrossed (and so morally blind and ethically uninvolved or incompetent) because of the slow yet relentless waning of the collectivities to be solidary with. It is because there is little reason to be solidary, "the others" turn into strangers—and of the strangers, as every mother keeps telling her child, one should beware; and best of all keep one's distance and not talk to them at all.[12]

Modern ways of life structure our perceptions of one another and disable us in various ways from handling common problems.

Addressing exactly these issues, democratic professionals want to open up environments that have become sealed off to meaningful lay citizen agency. Their aim is to share power over tasks and responsibility for problems they cannot fully handle on their own. In the process, they bring citizens together in a partially voluntary way: they create pressures and routines that encourage face-to-face contact and communication across major social differences. In other words, they rationally disorganize institutions and practices to foster routine, everyday democratic agency. In doing so, they develop a culture of responsibility for others.

Proximity and Responsibility

Bringing laypeople together to produce justice, education, public health and safety, and government—when done routinely in the normal social environment—helps backfill the erosion of contemporary public life. In part, it is accomplished by repairing our frayed participatory infrastructure: the traditional town meetings, public hearings, jury trials, and citizen oversight committees. It also requires remodeling these old forms and creating new civic spaces. Democratic professionals who share load-bearing work in schools, public health clinics, city governments, and even prisons are innovators who are expanding, not just conserving, American democracy.

Managers, officials, and midlevel professionals all too easily seal themselves off from clients, taxpayers, and patients; they serve and treat people without fully understanding them. They privilege speed, efficiency, and cost containment and employ hierarchies and divisions of labor. These internal arrangements create distance between organizations and citizens, neglecting the democratic value of proximity. To restore it, institutions must edge closer to the public work already being done by lay citizens and community groups. To borrow concepts from Max Weber, proximity requires adjusting formal institutional rationality to accommodate, appreciate, and act upon the substantive rationality of citizens.[13]

David Mathews aptly calls this process *alignment* and has shown how institutions and citizens alike gain from collaborative rather than technocratic working relations.[14] Alignment, Mathews points out, demands more than being "accountable," or "transparent," or "professional" to citizens on terms defined by professionals, but it "doesn't require massive reform or asking overworked professionals to take on an extra load of new duties."[15] Rather, it means an organization must rethink a social trustee orientation and recognize the value of citizens' attempts to solve problems on their own. Given the right kind of institutional culture, alignment can result in some organizational activities actually being steered by values and objectives brought in by laypeople. Stoicovy's democratic school in State College aligns to the issues and concerns brought in by active students empowered to use their voice. Abramson's community justice conferences in Baltimore align the criminal justice process to the contours of particular neighborhood conflicts.

Payne's study circles revealed practical ideas for dealing with longstanding issues of racial injustice in Lynchburg's local government. In each of these cases, too, alignment of an institutional world to the social and personal worlds gives meaning to citizen agency and challenges people to see one another as fellow citizens.

Proximity also involves bringing citizens together who had not planned to be together, had not joined a group or party or network. Kids in Stoicovy's school are students, not party members; participants in Abramson's conferences are neighbors, not association members; attendees at Payne's racial justice study circles are citizens, not advocates. Sometimes the substantive rationality that serves as a valuable corrective to technocratic or instrumental rationality doesn't arise from citizens' fully formed intentions and interests. Instead, it develops within institutions, through practices that encourage lay involvement and power-sharing. This sort of action is particularly important for treating issues people would rather ignore because they think they have no direct interest at stake or because they conceive of them as shameful or distasteful in some way—such as incarceration rates or prison conditions, for example. Proximity encourages coownership of processes, problems, and solutions that usually fall to the experts to handle. And it's precisely the fact that citizens neither demand nor desire coownership (at least in some cases) which makes proximity so important as a force for democratic change. Coownership is a bulwark against apathy and learned civic irresponsibility.

This latter kind of proximity, which brings previously unnetworked citizens together face-to-face, is less commonly discussed as relevant to democratization than the former type, which seeks to close the distance between citizens and institutions. So, it may help to say more about how, exactly, this interpersonal proximity works and why its effects would be discernibly democratic. Consider the capital jury, the body that must decide whether a death sentence is appropriate. Even though they seat only death-qualified jurors who believe the penalty is just in principle, such juries choose death significantly less often than the public-opinion statistics on Americans' views of the death penalty would predict.[16] It is not discourse about the validity of the death penalty or consciousness-raising that causes this discrepancy, but rather shared responsibility for a grave decision and proximity to the living, breathing person being sentenced. Likewise, standard Gallup-style public opinion polls about punishment in the United States register generally severe attitudes, but when more qualitative researchers provide context-rich narrative descriptions of particular offenders, respondents' sentencing opinions become more moderate.[17]

We have an underutilized capacity to connect, to see humanity even in the darkest corners of public life, to find common cause across our many legitimate differences and allegiances. It may be utopian to think that sharing public responsibility in public spaces will lead to robustly communitarian civic relationships, but perhaps it is enough if these serve as an antidote to the bureaucracy, compartmentalization of responsibility, and division of labor that make it difficult to recognize other people not like us as our fellow citizens.[18] As we see in the capital jury example, these juries are a way that courts share responsibility for justice; they circulate laypeople into a professionalized institution, and through the unanimity rule, make sure everyone's voice matters in a structured, sober, and reflective way. Fellow citizens sit in judgment regarding other citizens at their worst moments.

Likewise, we need to see our institutions as fields of social action, as our coproductions rather than as fixed forms. To do this, however, we must get them to stop thinking and acting for us. This is a job for democratic professionals, so therefore it is a job for those of us entering professions to think critically and energetically about the ways professional work blocks rather than fosters proximity. It is also a job for citizens to hold professionals and professionalized public institutions to higher, more participatory, standards. These are really big jobs, as we will see, because our institutions often do not want us to be too involved in the work they do for us.

:::::::::::
:::::::::::

III

Why Are Public Institutions Repellent to Citizen Agency?

Bearing Up, Taking On, Throwing Over, and Reconstructing

This country has a long history of democratic eruptions, but it is worth noticing how constructive many have been. Americans have borne up with systemic injustice, threats to the common good, and entrenched hierarchies, but then taken them on, thrown them over, and then built or reconstructed institutions to serve as preventatives.

Eighteenth-century revolutionaries remade the colonial institutions they had come to detest. They moved capitols to the centers of their states, refashioned legislative bodies so a broader swath of the population could stand for office, trimmed executive powers, and ensconced the participatory institution of the jury at the heart of the least participatory branch of government. Nineteenth-century abolitionists took on and threw over the wretched institution of slavery that had brutalized slaves and dehumanized slave-owners and passive onlookers alike. Late-nineteenth- and early-twentieth-century populists and progressives fundamentally reshaped public institutions held in sway by corporate interests, using initiative and recall devices. Later in the twentieth century, the civil rights and women's movements similarly worked from within the system through legal challenges.

My point is not to present a Whig historical sketch that glosses over conflict, fissures in the body politic, or chronic, persistent institutional failures, especially with respect to subgroups. Nor do I think any of our previous epochs was a civic Eden—a golden age of participation. Rather, I want to stress that twenty-first-century Americans are no less fed up with their institutions. We know from this history of bearing up, taking on, and throwing over that even institutions propped up by ancient assumptions are vulnerable to change. Yet, though there are eruptions of dissent today, beneath this surface protest we lack a constructive spirit of rebuilding. We seem stymied by how concrete our institutions are, how amorphous the public can be, how dependent we are on faceless systems for ordering our social world and helping us become the people we wish to be. There is a civic lethargy afoot in the land, and our institutions like it that way.

The Two Faces of Institutions

L ike most kids growing up in the 1970s, I quickly became aware of institutional power and savvy to the ways it could create and destroy. In grade school, I deeply admired the previous generations' scientific achievements such as the moon landing, while viscerally fearing and resenting others, like the prospect of nuclear annihilation. As an undergraduate, I studied the Robber's Cave and Stanford Prison experiments, which showed how institutional labels—in-group or out-group, guard or prisoner—could strongly influence how students just like me could generate solidarity while treating others as enemies and subhumans.

Institutions bring out our best and our worst. They help us form and maintain intimate attachments, organize and apply scientific knowledge, produce and deliver goods and services, and enact the very rules we live by. Yes, they may be complex, but this complexity helps us grow as individuals and as a society. Think of playing first violin on a Brandenburg Concerto without an orchestra, a music education, and many years of patterned practice. Or try to imagine interstate highways, stable financial markets, or widely accessible schools and universities without the public funding, regulation, and focused planning made possible by government.

Yet institutions can also be profoundly negative influences in our lives. Twenty-five years ago, Robert Bellah and his coauthors argued that American institutions were seriously dysfunctional. "Democracy means paying attention," they wrote, and American democracy had not been paying much attention—to the way government, work, and even family structures had become "corrupt; means have wrongly been turned into ends," in particular the ends of narrow economic success and individual fulfillment.[19] When they are saturated by values of the marketplace, or by patriarchy or racism or homophobia, our families, jobs, and laws will be correspondingly affected. Institutions focus our attention, sometimes on the wrong things:

> We live in and through institutions. The nature of the institutions we both inhabit and transform has much to do with our capacity to sustain attention. We could even say that institutions are socially organized forms of paying attention or attending, although they can also, unfortunately, be socially organized forms of distraction.[20]

Bellah et al.'s argument is a deep critique of the cognitive, moral, and civic barriers institutions pose to the realization of American democracy: "Because we have let too much of our lives be determined by processes 'going on over our heads,' we have settled for easy measures that have distracted us from what needs to be attended to and cared for."[21] Beneath the surface of democratic politics—which can erupt as it is in our time in waves of dissent and protest—there is an institutional layer constraining our ability to focus and work effectively together on major problems. If we care about improving our democracy, this layer in which many of us spend much of our working lives should be a primary focus: How can we find ways to share professionalized tasks with outsiders, listen to them, and engage their concerns, and how can we encourage professionals on the inside to listen and work with us? This strategy of institutional coproduction and collaboration may be more effective in the long term than a more "fugitive" politics of resistance.

Sociologists and others who study institutions think of them as stable arrangements that guide our actions and comport with communal values.[22] Institutions emerge to accomplish tasks that would be difficult to manage in a more inchoate or ad hoc fashion, such as to help us cope with the grief and loss and conflicts that are part of human social life as well as our needs for nurturing and healing and respect, but they do so in a way that inevitably reflects the values and commitments of the social order in which they are embedded.[23] Marriage and family life, the practice of medicine, the meting out of justice, and the education of the next generation, among many other undertakings, are all institutionalized, and they all reflect social norms regarding proper relationships, roles, and interactions; they exist to make certain actions easier and others harder.

Even though most institutions are public to some degree, in that they are socially embedded, we can differentiate some as *public institutions* when they produce nondivisible common goods such as public safety, are supported by public revenues, and are managed by people held publically accountable. Private institutions, by contrast, produce private goods—as when a private security force protects only certain individuals, paid for and held accountable primarily to a subgroup like a homeowners' association. The public nature of an institution places a special burden on it to install and heed public procedures of accountability that can determine whether the institution is, in fact, infused with widely shared values.

However, the special burden tends to be rather lightly felt. Sociological research on institutions shows how the rules and offices that impose useful regularity can also conflict with intended values. One famous study of democratic organizations found that institutional delegation of authority and division of labor led to concentrations of power that violated the groups' value commitments to equality. "Who says organization," Robert Michels chillingly wrote, "says oligarchy."[24] He thought these power-concentrating tendencies strong enough to call them "iron laws," although contemporary scholars dispute their strength and universality.[25] Yet even if they are not iron or ever-present, the propensities of institutions to align themselves toward internal rather than external purposes are powerful and common enough to pose problems.

Even more troublesome than the ways institutions violate their own core values are the barriers they place on thought.

While it is true that institutions are social creations, it is also true that they powerfully shape how we think about them, and indeed who we are. This is not a matter of corrupt institutions or power-hungry elites; it is standard operating practice. "How can we possibly think of ourselves in society," writes Mary Douglas, "except by using the classifications established in our institutions?"[26] "They fix processes that are essentially dynamic, they hide their influence, and they rouse our emotions to a standardized pitch on standardized issues."[27] This is just what institutions are for: they label, classify, and order. They think for us. As Douglas puts it, "The instituted community blocks personal curiosity, organizes public memory, and heroically imposes certainty on uncertainty."[28] Our dependence on institutions to tell us when we are "smart," and "capable," and "educated," for example, helps explain some of our anxiety about getting into exactly the best college and securing the right kind of degree; the better the college we are in, the "smarter," the more "capable," and the better "educated" we must, inevitably, be. Institutions, in fact, provide social validation and meaning for people—a student once told me he wanted to be a lawyer so he could wear a suit to work every day. Yet we need to be more reflective about the ways our institutions produce barriers to how we see and experience other people. Wear the suit, be validated, but also try your best to notice how your institutional world invalidates and clothes marginalized others in very different kinds of outfits.

Especially important is how institutions can think for us in ways that extract what are really complex moral choices about complicated human beings and replace them with sheer process, thus deflecting concern for others. They can strip away aspects of human beings that make a person familiar, replacing them with other features that make it harder for bureaucrats and officials to recognize and act on a responsibility to safeguard people's welfare inside and outside the institution. Zygmunt Bauman has called this the "management of morality," occurring in modern institutions through the "social production of distance, which either annuls or weakens the pressure of moral responsibility," the "substitution of technical for moral responsibility, which effectively conceals the moral significance of the action," and through "the technology of segregation and separation, which promotes indifference to the plight of the Other which otherwise would be subject to moral evaluation and morally motivated response."[29]

The institutional management of morality occurs quite straightforwardly and without a moment's notice in professionalized domains like health, education, criminal justice, and government. In criminal justice, for example, people are distanced from their law-abiding fellow citizens and treated in a technical rather than moral fashion as soon as they are suspects, a process that continues as defendants are given a case number and finally compelled to wear orange jumpsuits and shackles in court. Such management of morality is normal for institutions that handle a large volume of human business: complex men and women turn into clearances, caseloads, and dockets. The very "language in which things happen to them," writes Bauman, "safeguards its referents from ethical evaluation."[30] These linguistic and material forces of separation are even stronger with respect to human beings accused of harming others. By the very accusation, they have already become a candidate for expulsion from the warm "circle of proximity where moral responsibility rules supreme."[31]

Repellent Institutions

In addition to doing our thinking for us and shaping how we perceive those they have a hold of, many institutions repel public examination and participation in three distinct ways. Staying with the example of criminal justice, consider how much of the work being done is physically removed from both the lay public and any official not directly involved with trying a defendant, caring for a prisoner, or guiding a parolee. Erving Goffman called prisons "total institutions" because they are separate and complete worlds for those inside; communication and interaction with those outside, indeed even visibility, are all tightly circumscribed and controlled.[32] The work of administering criminal justice—handling the content of probation orders, among other tasks—is normally conducted outside the public by-ways. To use an example I already mentioned, mandated courses on life skills, anger management, and the like are often held in buildings and sites lacking any exterior signs communicating that something relevant to the public is happening inside. Court professionals' reliance on plea bargaining means very few criminal cases ever go to public trial. Even when there are trials, many jurors find them bureaucratic and oddly disempowering.[33]

Second, criminal justice institutions repel public examination and participation because of their sheer complexity. As Lucia Zedner points out, the common phrase "criminal justice system" should be resisted "on the grounds that this label masks its plural, disparate, even chaotic, character."[34] What is really a "series of largely independent organizations with differing cultures, professional ethos, and practices" is not easy even for practitioners to understand, much less members of the lay public.[35] In his critique of the kind of structured distraction that permitted America's steep rise in incarceration, William Stuntz indicates how a many-handed decision-making process thwarted the assessment of responsibility:

> Where state and local officials alike were responsible for rising levels of imprisonment, neither was truly responsible. Prosecutors sent more and more defendants to state prisons in part because state legislators kept building more prison cells. . . . For their part, the

legislators kept adding to their state's stock of prison beds because local prosecutors kept sending defendants to state prisons: if they're coming, you must build it. Neither set of officials fully controlled the process by which those prison beds were made and filled, so neither was able to slow or reverse that process. And the voters with the largest stake in that process—chiefly African American residents of high-crime city neighborhoods—had the smallest voice in the relevant decisions.[36]

Thus, even the officials and professionals involved in specific decisions at one level cannot be said to plan, intend, or even fully comprehend the cumulative institutional consequences of their actions.

Third, and most subtly, criminal justice institutions repel public awareness and involvement because they perform and characterize tasks in ways that neutralize the public's role. Critics advocating a more "restorative" approach have argued that criminal justice institutions "steal conflicts" and have "a monopoly on justice."[37] These are dramatic ways of saying something quite uncontroversial, namely, that most public institutions have something to prove: that they are the experts in providing health care, justice, information gathering or education, thus justifying why each respective institution deserves to expand its budget and authority to tackle social problems. In fact, institutions are constantly in competition with noninstitutional modes of accomplishing the same goals and thus have a tendency to characterize social problems in ways they can manage. State institutions in particular, by monopolizing coercive force, can make it seem that they are the difference between order and chaos, yet this is an illusion. Informal social control is far more important than the formal coercive measures criminal justice institutions deliver, and yet our public discourse—influenced by the ways our institutions think for us—construes courts, prisons, and probation officers as the active agents—and families, neighborhoods, and civil associations as passive recipients of crime control benefits produced by institutions.[38]

Yet perhaps we should just shruggingly acknowledge the ways institutions think and act for us as simply part of modern life. We are surrounded, after all, by complex and quasi-autonomous systems such as financial markets, so why is it surprising or troubling that public institutions are also complex and quasi-autonomous?

Here we must draw a normative distinction between institutions that require greater public steering and those that do not. Some institutions have clearly defined and uncontroversial objectives, the pursuit of which is easily monitored. Civil engineering agencies that plan and build highways, sewers, or airports may not always require regular and significant public engagement. Other institutions are charged with tasks that do not have discernible, long-lasting, negative effects on human lives. The Bureau of Weights and Measures no doubt influences how we count and calculate, but it does not appear to hold much risk of impairing people's lives. By contrast, it should be obvious that institutions like criminal justice, health care, and education lack clearly defined, uncontroversial, and easily monitored objectives, and at the same time pose enormous risks for impairing human development if their work is done poorly or unfairly.

Although they are complex and quasi-autonomous, public institutions cannot function without taxpayer support. They often operate under the oversight of managers selected by officials elected in free, competitive elections, and they purport to deliver goods like education, health, and public safety. Although they frequently resist or repel public responsibility, they are nevertheless the public's responsibility. To put it plainly, the public needs to better own up to the work being done by their institutions. Wherever core values are plural and contested, wherever neglectful or uncaring policies and practices have severe consequences, and wherever an institution depends upon the public to function, the work is our responsibility. If we are to have public institutions at all, we must hold ourselves accountable for what they do and for the reasons behind their actions.

My view differs somewhat from similar arguments distinguishing legitimate from illegitimate institutions. Legitimacy arguments valorize consent: subjects of rules or laws should have a concrete and not merely symbolic role in authorizing them and should understand what they must obey. Yet

I think being part of a good institution means more than making sure its rules and laws serve your own interests. I favor a broader conception of collective self-government: good institutions allow you to influence and help steer the powers to which you contribute and which speak and operate in your name, but they also call you to account for how they treat other people not like you, and when needed, to stand up and address discriminatory or repressive or otherwise inhumane practices. When institutions distance the work of education, health care, and criminal justice from lay citizens, we may become unknowing supporters of rules or laws that affect people differently—some well, others poorly; some fairly, others unfairly. Think of how like sleepwalkers most Americans went about their daily routines for decades while our country became what Nils Christie called the "world champion of incarceration," by locking up a greater percentage of our citizens than any other democracy, with glaring racial disparities, brutal conditions, and staggeringly long sentences for some. While such a lack of awareness, reinforced by and indeed produced by modern institutions, can harm our personal interests, what troubles me is the lack of concern for others it permits. I think the problem is not merely the individual risks posed by the public institutions we choose not to steer, but the difficulties such a diffuse and quasi-autonomous system presents in holding each other accountable for our laws and how they affect others who are not like us.

Institutionally fostered public ignorance and civic lethargy turns citizen-beneficiaries into collaborationists. We must, as laypeople, become more inquisitive and more alert to what our institutions do and how they do it; we must, as professionals and professionals in training, be more creative about aligning them to communities while constructing access points for citizen agency and platforms for citizens to think together in close proximity. Otherwise our misaligned institutions will continue operating under their proximity deficits and serve as powerful counterdemocratic forces in the background of all our social and political reform efforts.

IV

Thinking (and Acting) for Ourselves: Rebuilding Public Institutions

The sort of participatory democracy we are discussing here is not anti-institution—320 million people live in the United States, after all. It simply requires a more central place for human contact and particularized responsibility. We must rationally disorganize our way back into our institutions, and innovative democratic professionals can help us learn how. In Vanessa Gray's and Donnan Stoicovy's democratic schools, for example, there are routine opportunities for students to solve administrative problems, develop ongoing rules, and shape the curriculum. Education, to some degree, is not delivered to them; they are coproducing it. Their educational institutions are not thinking and acting for them, but with them.

Participatory democracy is thus not just more people acting all the time, nor is it about fixing ignorant and uncaring citizens. It is about building access points, forging alignment, fostering proximity, and infusing citizen agency at critical junctures throughout all of our public institutions. The kind of citizen–professional collaborations democratic professionals aim to foster directly address and reform the kinds of counterdemocratic tendencies and asocial structures that reinforce callousness and make social problems difficult to handle.

Let's consider the case of criminal justice reform. Criminal justice institutions are both more and less impervious to democratic innovation than they seem at first glance. They are more resistant, despite the inherently public nature of their task, because of the many ways they repel public awareness and involvement. We have just seen how the institutional environment of policing, prosecution, plea bargaining, and imprisonment is largely nontransparent, hierarchical, and nonparticipatory. Nevertheless, as we have also seen, the criminal justice system is not really a "system" and therefore contains multiple access points for innovation. Moreover, criminal justice happens in many rooms: at the police department, in the prosecutor's office, and in the courtroom, of course, but also on the school playground, where everyday conflicts are worked on by students themselves. So many of these other quasi-formal sites exist in our world—places in which tensions, problems, and frictions can receive the hearing and settlement they deserve.

Motivations for Reform

It is worth pointing out that motivations for reform are present on the inside and outside of mainstream institutions, and there's a palpable sense of urgency about racially biased patterns of policing, adjudicating, and punishing.

On the inside, the institutional failings are widely acknowledged. Think back to former attorney general Eric Holder's remark a few years ago that his colleagues need to be "smarter on crime," meaning more sensible about sentencing for nonviolent or low-level offenses and more conscious of the racial biases of current practice.[39] Though Holder applauded his colleagues' professionalism, "smarter on crime" means at least some of them have been kind of dumb. Holder's remarks were just the most prominent instance of professional self-criticism pointing to how criminal justice institutions are out of alignment with victims, offenders, and communities.

On the outside, we see citizens' movements calling for changes—in policing, specifically, but also to address racial inequality in sentencing, the overuse of incarceration, inhumane prison conditions, and the degraded civic status of ex-offenders. Street activism, large-scale social networking, and citizen journalism have made some significant headway: they have produced increased mainstream media awareness, commitments to reform from prominent officials, and a number of specific, concrete changes like increased use of body cameras. So, the insiders have felt great pressure for reform from the outsiders.

But street activism fades. People have to go back to their jobs and their families. And the very same repellent barriers reassert themselves, institutions seal back up again, and they resume thinking and acting for us. The good-hearted professionals on the inside say, "We will clean up our act, we will be smarter on crime," and the good-hearted activists on the outside say, "We will come back and protest unless you do," but something is missing. Neither inside reformers nor outside activists have fully grappled with how resistant—at a deep structural level—criminal justice institutions are to citizen agency and thus to lasting transformation. Beyond a change in official attitudes, some firings here and a new policy there, what is needed, I think, is a greater sense of public ownership of the harmful situations and conflicts that get translated into crimes.

This is where democratic professional efforts play a constructive role. Participatory innovations in local governments, schools, prisons, and community organizations can bring people—who may rather be doing something else—into the work of criminal justice. These are efforts in power-sharing, but they also have to do with learning to care about what is happening to people around you, and taking some responsibility, some share of public ownership, for social ordering and repair. Moreover, lessons learned by participatory innovators in criminal justice have much to teach reformers in other institutional fields.

Five Sites of Ongoing Democratic Innovation in Criminal Justice

Power sharing has been a long-standing part of American criminal justice through the jury system. Though it handles only a small fraction of criminal cases processed by the courts today, the jury's constitutional entrenchment and strong public support hold promise for democratic reformers. Some advocate increasing the number of trials by interrupting the plea-bargaining process (the primary cause of the jury's decline); others seek to reduce the jury's temporal and monetary costs to make it more attractive to court professionals. Also relevant are reforms intended to empower jurors to ask questions during the trial and not merely during deliberations, and allow juries a degree of sentencing authority after reaching a verdict. Though such reforms are marginal to everyday practice in most jurisdictions, a growing body of sympathetic court professionals embrace them, knowing that serious repairs need to be made if the jury system is to survive.[40]

A second site of increased citizen participation is the prison. Despite severe limits on lay citizen involvement in prisons, there are many ways for innovative professionals to open up these restrictive environments from the inside and demand access points from the outside. Prison education programs like Inside-Out, which link college and university teachers and students with groups of current prisoners, do more than provide educational opportunities for inmates; they create spaces for public dialogue about prison life and the reality of punishment. These credit-bearing courses bring college students together with an equivalent number of inmates for a few hours every week for one semester. They participate as fellow members of the same class, usually focused on issues of criminal justice, and work together on a class project. Other arrangements between universities and prisons have emerged organically using the Inside-Out model as a starting point. At Vanderbilt University, connections made during a prison reading group catalyzed work outside: an art show held on campus exhibited work done by the inmates in the group, campus workshops and conferences discussed mass incarceration, and community organizers took up the death penalty as an issue.[41] Also relevant here are efforts at promoting inmate advisory councils that can give voice to concerns about the prison administration.[42]

Police departments are a third site of innovation. Community policing efforts across the country involve advisory bodies composed of citizens who meet regularly in an evaluative and problem-solving capacity. The community beat meetings held by the Chicago Police Department, for example, create channels of communication between officers— who make the all-important street-level decisions that open the gates of the criminal justice process—and residents of neighborhoods affected by both crime and incarceration. Facilitated by civilians, these meetings bring residents together monthly with the police officers who patrol their neighborhoods. There, citizens can express their concerns about gangs, violence, theft, social disorder, dilapidated and abandoned buildings, traffic, parking, and even the competence and conduct of the police. Citizens also learn about the progress or lack thereof on past issues, and they can brainstorm other solutions.[43] These advisory bodies are present in other institutional locations, too, such as the community prosecution efforts in Portland, Denver, Indianapolis, and elsewhere, through which people can bring community issues to the attention of prosecutors and offer insights into what priorities are most important.

A fourth site of innovation is found in restorative justice programs. Present in every state in the United States, though most widely used in a handful of states—California, Pennsylvania, Minnesota, Texas, Colorado, Arizona, New York, Ohio, and Alaska—restorative justice programs have been housed in mayors' offices, lower courts, prosecutors' offices, departments of corrections, and in nongovernmental community organizations. Community Reparative Boards in Vermont, for example, are staffed by citizen volunteers and hold their meetings in public places like libraries, community centers, town halls, and police stations.[44] They conduct dialogues with offenders convicted but not sentenced for nonviolent offenses like underage drinking, impaired driving, and shoplifting. They seek to communicate the meaning of the harm for any victims involved, to determine how to repair whatever damage was done, and to consider how to avoid such action in the future. The outcome of dialogues is a contract with offenders involving community service, reparation, apologies, and the like. Other highly participatory programs, like Lauren Abramson's Community Conferencing Center in Baltimore, respond to referrals from police, prosecutors, schools, and community organizations by conducting neighborhood dialogues concerning conflicts that have not yet become institutionally labeled as formal offenses.[45]

Fifth, and finally, to turn full circle back to the site where this essay began, are the participatory conflict resolution practices found in some schools. Early experience with norm formation and social ordering may not have to resemble typical adult adjudication to nurture civic capabilities. Vivian Gussin Paley, for example, noticed that popular students in her Chicago primary school classroom had a surplus of playmates at recess while others, much to their shame and disappointment, were constantly excluded. After meetings with the children, Paley and the youth formulated a simple rule: "You Can't Say You Can't Play." Marginalized children could present this rule to those in more popular groups in order to gain admission to games they would normally have to witness from the sidelines. By taking part in rule-making and rule-enforcement, moreover, these children learned lessons in self-governance and participatory social control.[46] Another example comes from the Bathroom Busters, a group of St. Paul middle schoolers troubled by restrooms covered in graffiti, lacking in privacy because of broken stalls, and chronically short of soap and paper. Through the innovative Public Achievement program, they learned how to work with an inefficient school bureaucracy and to communicate with parents, teachers, and administrators to gain the resources needed to repaint walls, repair missing stall doors, and replenish needed supplies.[47] A problem that might have been seen as a juvenile offense, to be handled by school administrators and police officers, was translated into a social problem taken up by the students who refused to have professionals and institutions think and act for them.

These innovations are disruptive and constructive. They challenge the idea of criminal justice as a matter to be handled by an authoritative, professionalized body deciding guilt and measuring out punishment. Each in its own way reconstructs criminal justice as a multifaceted process encouraging thinking together about our conflicts, our harmful acts, and what we can do together to repair and prevent them. To do criminal justice in a participatory democracy is to move beyond "locking up the bad guys"; it is to try to do a better job of ordering our social world. This kind of thoughtful and responsible action begins as early as elementary school, is called for periodically even if we have not chosen to participate, brings us into close contact with people who differ from us, refuses to segregate those judged from those judging, and contributes to a public culture that is able to see, hear, think, and talk about difficult subjects.

Democratic innovations like these have found support from communitarian legal scholars stressing the advantages of civil society over formal institutions and from procedural justice researchers linking levels of citizen trust to transparent and responsive policing. Yet significant skepticism about the idea of democratizing criminal justice persists among scholars and activists who argue, from a social justice perspective, that under conditions of severe racial inequality, any attempt at reform that does not seek racial justice as a primary goal will fail, and among abolitionists claiming that punishment is always coercive, degrading, and therefore necessarily incompatible with true democracy.[48]

While these perspectives help us see what a more democratic form of criminal justice might look like, I want to reiterate a fundamental point about collective self-governance. Working through social problems with officials and formal institutions rather than having them think and act for us helps us live in a democracy that mindfully and responsibly handles chronic human difficulties. Between the communitarian position that "the people" can resolve conflicts and penalize in less-biased ways than officials, and the social justice and abolitionist position that they cannot, is the participatory democratic position I favor: citizens become "the people"—namely, become more sensitive to each other's requirements, more attentive to inequalities, disparities, and miseries—if and only if they work together on common problems like social ordering.

As Nils Christie said more than a quarter century ago in his great participatory democratic manifesto, "Conflicts as Property," "Conflicts represent one of the many cases of lost opportunities for involving citizens in tasks that are of immediate importance to them. This loss is first and foremost a loss in *opportunities for norm-clarification.* It is a loss of pedagogical possibilities. It is a loss in opportunities for a continuous discussion of what represents the law of the land."[49] Like Christie, I think the ability of citizens and professionals to collaborate together on social problems is a measure of our moral and political maturity.

∙∙∙∙∙∙∙∙∙∙
∙∙∙∙∙∙∙∙∙∙
∙∙∙∙∙∙∙∙∙∙

V

Growing Cultures of
Participatory Innovation

Showing up for a community justice conference, a prison discussion group, or a conflict-resolution program for a fifth-grade classroom may seem trivial, given that the bulk of decision making in criminal justice institutions proceeds in a relatively nonparticipatory fashion. It can, however, make a difference.

Restorative justice volunteers, beat meeting participants, and schoolchildren repairing breaches in social order on their own have real existence in political space and time. They are load-bearing members of the manifold institutions of criminal justice: the particular institutions they are working with are thinking and then acting through them. These innovations address what Margaret Urban Walker calls our "morally significant non-perception": the ways mainstream practices shield the advantaged from the consequences of policies like the draconian criminalization of certain drugs that has sent so many citizens to prison.[50] Normal, consistent citizen action inside and outside is required for contemporary publics to soberly acknowledge and assume responsibility for criminal justice institutions and for all public institutions oriented by plural and contested values and capable of doing great harm to human development.

Sparks of Democratic Energy
among Professionals

Democratic professionals bring laypeople together to make justice, education, public health, city government, and the like a regular part of the social environment. For these reformers, institutions are fields of democratic action produced by citizens acting together; they encourage and regulate action, to be sure, but they are not fixed forms. Yet what keeps innovators going when they hit obstacles or when resources needed to support their work dry up? How are others encouraged to take up similar projects?

What is fascinating but perhaps unsurprising is that the personal histories of many democratic professionals I have met reflect intense pessimism and disaffection with contemporary institutions. The schools, agencies, and programs for which they received work training appear to be controlled by untouchable forces of bureaucracy and managerialism. Moreover, these institutions seem to be failing to produce high-quality services and outcomes, and they do not treat people well as citizens or as human beings. Interviewees said that their traditional training set them up to be successful failures. They recognized that being the best conventional professional they could be was insufficient to rectify the problems plaguing these domains; and while this could have easily led to apathy, quietism, and careerism, it did not for them. The fighting creed of the democratic professional is the absolute refusal to perpetuate the dysfunctions of the currently dominant institutional environment. I have heard this sentiment expressed in numerous ways: *I refuse to reproduce schools, administrative offices, and government programs that do things* to *rather than* with *people, that disempower, that devalue or discourage lay contributions, that frustrate collaboration, that hinder collective work. I have one life, and with it, I will make my school, my office, my program a place of agency, of sharing, of dignity.*

As I interviewed Forest Grove principal Vanessa Gray about why she helped create a democratic school, it was clear she did not want to reproduce the institutional patterns of two other schools in her district. The high school is like a prison, she said, with a metal detector at the entrance and security cameras everywhere. In the elementary school, kids late to class are inked with a hand stamp in the image of a tortoise. Gray was not going to perpetuate a school culture that failed to treat people with dignity, as anything less than full citizens of the society they'd soon enter.

So, one motivating factor that keeps innovators alert and engaged in reform is a recognition of the institutional weaknesses in many domains, a kind of cultural embarrassment about reproducing practices that cause human suffering and generate inequality even as they purport to deliver a professional outcome: justice, education, information, health. With this recognition as well as awareness of participatory alternatives comes accountability: the belief that "we"—the ones with knowledge, or training, or simply the ambition to help solve social problems—can do better. Breaking down civic inequality and persistent, chronic divisions is what many went into their professional lives to accomplish. Participatory reforms in criminal justice and other domains allow professionals to live up to their own values and to be part of the solution to social problems rather than agents of their continued reproduction.

A related factor is the complexity of social problems and the absurdity of declaring professional jurisdiction over tasks traditionally claimed by social trustee forbears. This is clear in the "wicked problems" public administrators talk about: the policy areas such as substance abuse, urban poverty, and homelessness, which require a multifaceted—and indeed highly democratic—kind of professional collaboration to adequately comprehend, define, and address.[51] Yet it is increasingly clear that all traditional professional tasks are wicked in their own ways, as profession after profession is forced by circumstance to admit their limited grasp on complex problems: health requires not just good medical care but sound nutrition, which requires the elimination of food deserts; public safety requires not just good policing but communities attentive to broken windows; and on it goes. While it is still all too easy to respond to complexity by shoring up the symbols of social trustee professionalism and doubling down on managerial attitudes, declarations of vulnerability and invitations to collaborate appear commonly in the stories practitioners tell one another in professional meetings and training workshops about successful problem solving.

Barriers and Openings to Democratic Professionalism

Whether we are lay citizens, professionals, or professionals in training, we can each play a role in growing cultures of participatory innovation where we live and work. Our task will be helped along by sober recognition of both the obstacles in the path of innovations as well as some of the sources of support available along the way. Both barriers and openings for democracy exist in most professionalized domains.

As we've seen, democratic agency has some powerful barriers. Changes made by democratic professionals are more retail in nature than the wholesale changes sought by traditional social movement activists, yet they are not minor achievements. They manage to swim against some strong counterdemocratic currents: bureaucratic demands for efficiency, cost control, and clear chains of command; legal constraints that carve out specific zones of authority and responsibility; and economic incentives to assert jurisdictional control over certain problems, issues, and tasks.

Practitioners find opportunities for change as well as resources and allies. So-called wicked problems like obesity or substance abuse, which admit no unidimensional expert response, can prompt otherwise risk-averse public health professionals to collaborate with community members. Fixed and centralized government authority is given

Table 3: Barriers and openings for democracy in professionalized domains

Barriers	Openings
Jurisdictional claims of professions	"Wicked" cross-profession problems
Authority, responsibility, obligation	Division of labor and shared responsibility
Expertise	Local and social knowledge
Hierarchy and efficiency	Release of individual and group capacity

a reason to relax when participatory processes yield results by using local problem-solving knowledge. Hierarchy in schools, when it dampens students' powerful curiosity, sense of wonder, and love of inquiry, as many democratic teachers have discovered, can also loosen its organizational hold. More generally, too, widespread resentment of invasive, autonomy-threatening managerialism among skilled professionals motivates strategically useful allies in democratic culture change.

Participatory democracy has a major strategic advantage, too. These practitioners are enacting changes at the local and institutional levels that can improve lives immediately. By circumventing the slow wheels of legal or political machinery, their participatory innovations enable children to learn in more responsive schools, neighbors to take part in inclusionary community justice efforts, and prisoners to interact as citizens right away. Students, neighbors, and inmates improve their well-being at the very moment they conduct their work. Their collaborative, reflective, and at times load-bearing work can itself be a valuable end result.

Participatory innovation does not just happen naturally; it is part of many quiet struggles inside relatively closed institutions. In American K–12 education, for example, student participation in norm setting and adjudication is, in the words of student voice advocate Dana Mitra, "counternormative." Much more common is the top-down approach of the principal applying the rule and meting out a sanction. The ongoing struggle between these modes comes to the surface in debates over the hardening of school disciplinary sanctions against student norm-breakers and in discussions of alternative procedures such as restorative justice. Seemingly microscopic, trivial, and all-too-local from the perspective of traditional democratic theory, these are the small battles, I think, that will define future institutions as fields of self-government or will continue to reproduce the repellent status quo. Thus, I think more attention should be paid to what we might do—as citizens, academics, and fellow practitioners— to sustain and encourage people like Vanessa Gray and other innovators on the inside and outside of institutions who are making them more reflective and participatory.

It is commonplace to assert against arguments like mine that widespread lay participation is somehow too idealistic for the real world of heterogeneous publics and complex policy problems. I think this is wrong. In fact, I have found that collaboration and power-sharing efforts are frequently initiated when the going gets tough for city managers, school district leaders, and police chiefs. They find, in times of crisis, that rationally disorganized institutions are the way to regain public trust after a budget shortfall, police shooting, or school performance failure. It is the expert institution, sealed off from the public it is meant to serve, that is too pure for this modern world. Participatory innovators may be idealists, but they are also realists; they know the humanizing practices they seek to bring into currently closed and repellent institutional spaces are desperately needed in the real world.

There is a long way to go, of course, though it helps to think of participatory democracy not as a specific achievable goal but as a range of ongoing, open-ended, always-imperfect settlements as human beings seek to work out their problems together. Democratic professionalism may not be a typical social movement, but it could develop a critical mass. As democratic innovator Lauren Abramson notes, "Cultural change does not happen overnight. Restorative justice is like groundwater. Most people don't see groundwater, but it nourishes a lot of things. Eventually, it is going to bust through."[52]

Conclusion: Democratic Professionals on Campus?

You might have noticed that I did not mention universities when discussing growing cultures of participatory innovation. This could seem like an oversight, given how higher education institutions serve as gatekeepers to nearly every profession—and therefore as sites of possible leverage to help professions transition to a more democratic model. But universities are often as marked by the repellant, technocratic, and self-serving tendencies we have seen operative in other professional fields as by barriers to more participatory norms. With few exceptions, the democratic professionals I have met emerge despite their university training, not because of it.

People in Glass Houses

I became aware of the problem even before I started my research on innovative democratic professionals. For years

I have included on some of my syllabi the "Port Huron Statement" written by Tom Hayden and others in the Students for a Democratic Society. In this classic 1960s manifesto, Hayden advocates cooperative workplaces, open social relations, and citizen-oriented governing institutions. He urges his fellow students to recognize and make use of their universities as sites of transformative change: as models of participatory democracy and channels for transmitting these values into the outside world. Committed to collegiality and truth seeking, faculty listen to good reasons, and their seminars are places of critical dialogue in which students can challenge repressive, hierarchical, and self-interested practices on campus and in society at large, thus sensitizing and activating their fellows in close proximity in classrooms and campus gathering places. As graduates take their places in corporate and public worlds, they will incrementally remake the institutions therein in a more participatory democratic fashion.

Hayden's narrative pictures the university as more deeply egalitarian and invested in cultural change than it sometimes appears. Yet students in my seminars tend to be unmoved. They care about reforming institutions and are far from apathetic, but the trouble is that students recognize their university is less democratic than it seems on the surface and is therefore an unreliable platform for transformative change. Universities only appear to be collegial, yet in reality often have unaccountable hierarchical management structures.

Relying on private search firms, trustees choose presidents and provosts with scant authentic input from below; once ensconced, these top administrators are typically evaluated with relatively nontransparent and nonparticipatory procedures. Administrative professionalism tends to follow a full-fledged social trustee model, with faculty, student, and community opinion rarely consulted with any seriousness. The absence of a vibrant democratic professionalism is evident, too, in the classroom and in daily faculty–student noninteraction. Though research and disciplinary specialization are commonly blamed for these academic tendencies, the deeper problem is a proximity deficit: faculty members' inability to see and act with students as fellow citizens, as collaborators—if only neophytes—in a common public project of understanding and improving shared social, political, and economic structures.

To be better models of participatory democracy, universities must convey through their own practices that institutions are not impervious to change, but are composed of real people with discernment, agency, fallibility, and a willingness to work across disciplinary, managerial, and generational divisions. Core ingredients of a more democratic academic culture include a commitment to power sharing that in turn requires free speech, collegial respect, reciprocity, absence of unnecessary hierarchy, suspicion of lock-step proceduralism, and commitment to collective decision making. Though many American colleges and universities systemically fail to live up to these norms, which are overpowered by the institutional forces we have been talking about—bureaucracy, routinization, legal accountability, risk management, and market definitions of efficiency and productivity—there is no small number of students, faculty, and administrators seeking a more participatory culture.

Administrators who take up the challenge to become democratic professionals have a significant role to play in fostering dialogue with faculty and student committees with real responsibilities. For their part, faculty who accept the challenge can do much more to recognize students as cocreators of their education. Beyond receptivity to student voice and influence in seminars and in the shaping of curricula, there is the fundamental issue of how little time there is for research, student interaction, campus obligations, and work with community organizations. There is never enough time. To better model democratic practice, stakeholders need to find the time—fewer students per class, fewer classes per faculty member, fewer credits necessary to graduate—through some kind of calculus that respects research, students, and community.

Dangerous Outposts of a Humane Civilization?

Along with being more self-aware about their internal counterdemocratic tendencies, to be contributors rather than barriers to an emerging culture of participatory innovation, colleges and universities need to look more carefully into the ways they think about instruction in professional and skilled work. Are they fostering—through their conceptual models, disciplinary knowledge, and training programs—widespread citizen agency and democratic self-determination, or are they mostly cultivating their own? Without a doubt, campus "civic engagement" programs and offices are thriving, but they are often freewheels spinning alongside the university's driving imperatives, which remain squarely attached to the social trustee model of managerial, technocratic professionalism.

There are some very basic choices to be made: future criminal justice professionals, for example, can be taught to represent clients, deliver justice, and provide security to a largely passive populace, or they can be taught to include citizens and neighborhoods in cocreating a just social order. The social trustee status quo will persist by default as long as higher education professionals complacently fail to recognize the costs of business as usual, which are paid out in the counterdemocratic trends in contemporary institutions and concomitant levels of civic lethargy and public distrust. Students have a powerful role here, too, to question the professional fields many will enter upon leaving university: What skills am I acquiring that can help me succeed not only in terms of status and financial reward, but in working with future colleagues to do better than our predecessors in humanizing our public institutions?

There are openings for critically minded and constructive students to press these issues at many universities, to be sure, and there exist sparks of democratic energy among receptive professionals in a wide variety of academic, public, private, research, liberal arts, and specialized institutions across many disciplines. Yet it is an uphill struggle for students and faculty alike.[53] Many appear to be aware of the costs of the status quo, realizing the world the previous generation helped shape is one populated by providers and clients, producers and consumers, a world with profoundly undemocratic institutions that every day assert without even having to say it: "Lay citizens cannot do justice and cannot do public safety because we, the professionals, do that work for you." Internal problems plague mainstream professionalism, too, for institutions that treat people primarily as clients and consumers rather than active agents and partners do not adequately deliver goods like justice and public safety, and are unfulfilling to work in because they separate professionals from important social sources of emotional nourishment and practical local knowledge.

The democratic professionals I have met reject institutional hypocrisy: the school that says it is educating citizens while providing no opportunities for self-government, or the prison that is so closed off to the public world that it cannot provide an avenue back into society for norm-violators. Undergraduates, graduate students, and faculty working in the natural and social sciences, arts and humanities, law, education, medicine, and engineering struggle with a similar situation. What many of us find desirable about our academic work—the freedom to choose intellectual projects, the collaborative aspect of research, the power-sharing in a laboratory, institute, or department, and the horizontal learning as new cohorts circulate through campus—is just what is being squeezed out of the misaligned and counterdemocratic institutional domains we are unthinkingly supporting through our campuses' professional education and credentialing processes. We who administrate, teach, and study in professional education programs need to ask harder questions about what it means to be a professional today, and we need to seek some outside advice. Academics talk about the need for "public outreach" to spread ideas and best practices from the university out into the community; what I have in mind is the opposite. We need some "in-reach."

My suggestion here is humility. Academics are no vanguard, either in modeling best practices or offering theoretical models. We need to listen more, to take up the knowledge of people outside our normal disciplinary channels, to learn about the different modes of task-sharing, collaboration, coownership, and democratic divisions of labor that brilliant nonacademic innovators are manifesting in daily life. We can help them form networks to share information and build platforms for problem solving. By listening and learning, we can also incorporate some of their lessons of new democratic practice into higher education, striving toward the "dangerous outposts of a humane civilization" that Dewey hoped schools could become.[54]

Beyond Legislators and Interpreters: Doing Democratic Theory With and For

Focusing on the small territory of academia I live in called democratic theory, I want to conclude with some reflections on how people like me might do the kind of "in-reach" that could better relate to innovators. This is harder than it might seem. Writing and thinking are such solitary activities—democracy is not. Worse, time spent writing and thinking is surely time not spent in an elected office making decisions, or in a neighborhood organizing a collective effort, or in a public space articulating grievances. Democratic theory, therefore, is always working against itself to some extent; in only the barest, most abstract sense does it seek others outside the world of thinking and writing. And this may explain why the others outside are not seeking us much, either.

One of the most sobering insights gained indirectly through my research is how distant democratic theory is from the work of people who are good at doing democracy. They become as smart as they are about democracy by doing it, by reflecting on it with others, but—this is the sobering part—never by dwelling on the texts I cherish in the academic canon. Democratic professionals do their work without help from any theory that resembles what we academics write. Names instantly recognizable to political theorists draw blank looks. This suggests completely different fields of thought and action rather than one shared field that has only to overcome a barrier between theory and practice.

To face this problem squarely, I think, is to practice democratic theory as a catalytic rather than traditionally academic discipline—meaning that research is done with and for the people being studied. *With* means listening carefully to democratic innovators, correcting and adjusting conceptual frameworks as one goes along, and taking suggestions on other lines of inquiry. *For* means contributing somehow to the success of their work by broadcasting it, encouraging discussion, and making links across professional domains to grow and diversify networks. Such an unabashedly open-ended and reform-minded methodological stance is not the only way to do democratic theory, of course, but it seems an appropriate expression of academic democratic professionalism: an admission of intellectual fallibility, sensitivity to the power of naming, humility in constructing theoretical frameworks, a commitment to task-sharing in concept building, and solidarity with those engaged in the never-ending project of humanizing the institutional world we shape and are shaped by.

Zygmunt Bauman classified modern intellectuals into two categories: "legislators" and "interpreters."[55] The former is a rational planner who seeks to influence law, policy, and culture to shape productive and fulfilling lives and relationships. The latter—aware on the one hand of the failures of rational social planning, yet appreciative of the wild diversity of productive and fulfilling lives—eschews the planning and shaping role and takes up the task of learning about other ways of life, and then translates these so that people might understand one another better. As Bauman himself realized, neither type of intellectual seems to matter in contemporary life. The institutions are humming along without the services proffered by intellectuals, and the people purportedly in need of shaping or interpreting are not paying much attention, either.

Legislators and interpreters are both "meta-professionals," people specializing in reason and careful methods who are somehow above and beyond practitioners as well as those others who are merely living their lives. For those following a democratic professional rather than meta-professional path, however, I propose a third possibility: "active listeners." Active listeners do not build systems, yet we also do not just translate fixed meanings from one group to another; we are coequal—or try to be—in meaning making and system building. We open our ears, our eyes, our hearts, our minds, and we try to hear and see and feel and think more acutely, and, in our institution-shaping work and dialogue with others, we hold them to those expectations as well. We care about democracy, and we are troubled by the sneaky ways our own habits, norms, practices, and social structures on and off campus block and disable it.

I do not yet know how to make adequate use of active listening, nor what narrative forms are the best vehicles for it, but it is evident that some of the most practically useful and theoretically rich texts in democratic theory are fascinating hybrids written by active listeners—from Montesquieu's *Spirit of the Laws* to Tocqueville's *Democracy in America* to Dewey's *Democracy and Education* and Mansbridge's *Beyond Adversary Democracy*. We will notice more of the world of actual and potential democracy, I think, and understand more about what we might contribute to it, if we assume that knowledge is created together, that concepts and theories move forward in conjunction with ground-level awareness earned through qualitative and participatory action research. As readers, too, we should ask if there is room in a theory for us, for our experiences, abilities, ideas, fears, and hopes. Democratic theory should not legislate for us, nor merely interpret what we already know, but rather, invite us into the common project. Even in our anxious times, there is a world of democratic possibility to actively hear as we rebuild our public world—together.

Acknowledgments

M uch is owed to many, but I want to recognize a few
people and organizations for their particularly
important help in shaping the ideas presented here. First,
thanks are due to Peter Levine for nominating this research
for the award and to Harry Boyte and Ian Loader for their
letters of support. Peter and Harry are true pioneers in the
emerging field of civic studies; their work is of immense
value to those of us thinking about how to reconnect citizens to institutions. Ian's path-breaking research on democracy and criminal justice, often done in collaboration with
our mutual friend Richard Sparks, has been crucial to my
understanding of these issues.

I am grateful for the collegiality and support for public
scholarship provided by the Kettering Foundation. Visits to
the foundation allowed me test out unformed arguments and
gather evidence in workgroups made up of some of the most

constructively critical and democratic intellectuals I know. Thanks are due to Derek Barker, John Dedrick, and David Mathews for aiding and abetting.

For creating forums for my ongoing interviews with democratic professionals as well as for offering suggestions, prompts, and cues along the way, thanks are also due to thoughtful colleagues at the *Boston Review*, *The Good Society*, and *Restorative Justice: An International Journal.*

Finally, this essay could not have been written without the help of the innovators in the trenches—Lauren Abramson, Vanessa Gray, Kimball Payne, Donnan Stoicovy, among others—inviting us to join in the work that belongs to all of us, the work of creating a more attentive and humane democracy out of our sometimes inhospitable institutional environments.

Notes

1　David Mathews puts this point well when he writes about "a politics where citizens don't just comply or advise; they act. They get things done. They produce." *The Ecology of Democracy* (Dayton, OH: Kettering Foundation Press, 2014), 28.

2　See Theda Skocpol, *Diminished Democracy: From Membership to Management in American Civic Life* (Norman: University of Oklahoma Press, 2003).

3　Marc Galanter, "The Vanishing Trial: An Examination of Trials and Related Matters in Federal and State Courts," *Journal of Empirical Legal Studies* 1 (2004): 459–570.

4　See Steven Brint, *In an Age of Experts: The Changing Role of Professionals in Politics and Public Life* (Princeton, NJ: Princeton University Press, 1994).

5　Talcott Parsons, "Professions," in *International Encyclopedia of the Social Sciences*, vol. 12 (New York: Macmillan, 1968), 536.

6　See, e.g., Ivan Illich, *Medical Nemesis: The Expropriation of Health* (New York: Random House, 1976); Michel Foucault, "Truth and Juridical Forms," in *Essential Works of Foucault, 1954–1984*, vol. 3, eds. P. Rabinow and J. D. Faubion (New York: The New Press, 2000).

7   Sheldon Wolin, "Fugitive Democracy," *Constellations* 1 (1994).

8   See Albert W. Dzur, *Punishment, Participatory Democracy, and the Jury* (New York: Oxford University Press, 2012) for more on load-bearing participation.

9   Alexis de Tocqueville, *Democracy in America*, ed. Olivier Zunz, trans. Arthur Goldhammer (New York: The Library of America, 2004), 585–587.

10   John Dewey, *The Public and its Problems*, in *John Dewey, The Later Works: 1925–1953*, vol. 2, ed. J. A. Boydston (Carbondale: Southern Illinois University Press, 1981), 327.

11   Zygmunt Bauman, "Ethics of Individuals," *Canadian Journal of Sociology* 25 (2000): 86.

12   Bauman, "Ethics of Individuals," 87.

13   Max Weber, *Economy and Society*, ed. G. Roth and C. Wittich (Berkeley: University of California Press, 1978).

14   "Alignment occurs when gears mesh," writes Mathews, "when institutions and citizens work in a complementary, mutually reinforcing fashion. The work citizens do puts control in their hands, and it also benefits institutions. Institutions become more effective as they profit from the work of citizens. And they are likely to become more responsive when they see the benefits from this work." David Mathews, *The Ecology of Democracy*, 140.

15   Ibid., 142.

16   See James P. Levine, *Juries and Politics* (Belmont, CA: Wadsworth, 1992), 95. As Justice Stevens puts this point, "Voting for a political candidate who vows to be 'tough on crime' differs vastly from voting at the conclusion of an actual trial to condemn a specific individual to death." *Harris v. Alabama*, 513 U.S. 504, 518 (1995) (Stevens, J., dissenting).

17   See John Doble, "Attitudes to Punishment in the US—Punitive and Liberal Opinions," in *Changing Attitudes to Punishment*,

eds. J. Roberts and M. Hough (Portland, OR: Willan, 2002), 148–162. Julian Roberts calls the moderation of punitive attitudes after closer proximity to a specific offender "one of the most robust and often-replicated findings" in the field of criminal justice research. Julian Roberts, "The Future of State Punishment," in *Retributivism Has a Past: Has It a Future?* ed. M. Tonry (New York: Oxford University Press, 2011), 105.

18 Marc Stears has also called for more collaboration in workplaces and in public life. I share his goals, but disagree when he posits "relationships" as primary levers of change. I think we have found it hard enough to maintain *decent*—much less *friendly*—civic relationships across race, class, and education divisions. Collaborative work in public places can result in a sobering-up process, however, that calls our attention to other people not like us. Civic relationships can emerge, of course, but I think civic sobriety is a demanding-enough goal. See Stears, *Everyday Democracy: Taking Centre-Left Politics beyond State and Market* (London: Institute for Public Policy Research, 2011).

19 Robert Bellah, R. Madsen, W. M. Sullivan, A. Swidler, and S. M. Tipton, *The Good Society* (New York: Knopf, 1991), 291.

20 Ibid., 256.

21 Ibid., 273.

22 "The function of institutions is always the same," writes Talcott Parsons, a pioneer in this field, "the regulation of action in such a way as to keep it in relative conformity with the ultimate common values and value-attitudes of the community." Talcott Parsons, "Prolegomena to a Theory of Social Institutions," *American Sociological Review* 55 (1990): 331.

23 "To institutionalize," writes Philip Selznick, "is to infuse with value beyond the technical requirements of the task at hand." Philip Selznick, *The Moral Commonwealth: Social Theory and the Promise of Community* (Berkeley: University of California Press, 1992), 233.

24 Robert Michels, *Political Parties: A Sociological Study of the Oligarchical Tendencies of Modern Democracy* (Glencoe, IL: Free Press, 1962), 365.

25 See Ricardo Blaug, *How Power Corrupts: Cognition and Democracy in Organisations* (London: Macmillan, 2010). Blaug convincingly argues that conventional treatments of organizations in Michels and elsewhere have mistakenly naturalized hierarchy and have failed to capture its destabilizing and nonfunctional characteristics.

26 Mary Douglas, *How Institutions Think* (Syracuse, NY: Syracuse University Press, 1986), 99.

27 Ibid., 92.

28 Ibid., 102.

29 Zygmunt Bauman, *Modernity and the Holocaust* (London: Polity, 1989), 199.

30 Ibid., 103.

31 Ibid., 195.

32 Erving Goffman, *Asylums: Essays on the Social Situation of Mental Patients and Other Inmates* (Chicago, IL: Aldine, 1962).

33 See, e.g., D. G. Burnett, *A Trial by Jury* (New York: Vintage, 2001) on jury service as bureaucratic and disempowering, but note that Gastil et al. found jurors more likely to have a positive civic experience when they deliberate more, when the case they are adjudicating is complex—the more of a load they are expected to bear—and when they are treated well by court professionals. John E. Gastil, P. Deess, P. J. Weiser, and C. Simmons, *The Jury and Democracy: How Jury Deliberation Promotes Civic Engagement and Political Participation* (New York: Oxford University Press, 2010).

34 Lucia Zedner, "Reflections on Criminal Justice as a Social Institution," in *The Eternal Recurrence of Crime and Control: Essays*

in Honour of Paul Rock, eds. D. Downes, D. Hobbs, and T. Newburn (London: Oxford University Press, 2010), 71.

35 Ibid., 72.

36 William J. Stuntz, *The Collapse of American Criminal Justice* (Cambridge, MA: Harvard University Press, 2011), 255.

37 See Nils Christie, "Conflicts as Property," *British Journal of Criminology* 17 (1977): 2; and Howard Zehr, *Changing Lenses: A New Focus for Criminal Justice* (Scottdale, PA: Herald Press, 1990), 121.

38 The "vast majority of crime problems" are handled through "social policy and social institutions beyond the criminal process." Nicola Lacey, "Social Policy, Civil Society and the Institutions of Criminal Justice," *Australian Journal of Legal Philosophy* 26 (2001): 9. As Zedner puts it, "to assume that crime control is the prerogative of criminal justice agents and institutions obscures the role played in controlling crime by informal sources and institutions of social order—not least the family, the school, religious institutions, and the community. Such ability as criminal justice institutions have to tackle crime relies heavily upon these informal sources of order and their interdependent relationship with them." "Reflections on Criminal Justice as a Social Institution," 73.

39 Eric Holder, "Remarks at the Annual Meeting of the American Bar Association's House of Delegates," (San Francisco, CA, August 12, 2013). Available at http://www.justice.gov/opa/speech/attorney-general-eric-holder-delivers-remarks-annual-meeting-american-bar-associations.

40 See Symposium on Democratizing Criminal Justice, *Northwestern University Law Review,* vol. 111, special issue (2017).

41 See Albert W. Dzur, "Teaching Philosophy on Death Row: An Interview with Lisa Guenther," *Boston Review*. Available at http://www.bostonreview.net/blog/dzur-trench-democracy-1.

42 See Amy E. Lerman and Vesla Mae Weaver, "A Trade-Off between Safety and Democracy? An Empirical Investigation of Prison Violence and Inmate Self-Governance," in *Democratic Theory and Mass Incarceration*, eds. A. W. Dzur, I. Loader, and R. Sparks (Oxford: Oxford University Press, 2016).

43 Wesley Skogan, *Police and Community in Chicago: A Tale of Three Cities* (New York: Oxford University Press, 2006), p. 142.

44 See Albert W. Dzur, *Democratic Professionalism: Citizen Participation and the Reconstruction of Professional Ethics, Identity, and Practice* (University Park: Pennsylvania State University Press, 2008), ch. 6.

45 See Lauren Abramson and D. B. Moore, "Transforming Conflict in the Inner City: Community Conferencing in Baltimore," *Contemporary Justice Review* 4 (2001): 321–340.

46 Vivian Gussin Paley, *You Can't Say You Can't Play* (Cambridge, MA: Harvard University Press, 1992).

47 The middle schoolers were coached by University of Minnesota undergraduates involved in the Center for Democracy and Citizenship's Public Achievement program, which is strongly motivated by ideas of citizen agency and more democratic forms of professionalism. See Harry C. Boyte, *Everyday Politics: Reconnecting Citizens and Public Life* (Philadelphia: University of Pennsylvania Press, 2004).

48 See, e.g., the essays in Symposium on Democratizing Criminal Justice.

49 Christie, "Conflicts as Property," 7–8.

50 Walker, *Moral Understandings: A Feminist Study in Ethics*, 2nd ed. (New York: Oxford University Press, 2007).

51 On the concept of "wicked problems," see Horst W. J. Rittel and Melvin M. Webber, "Dilemmas in a General Theory of Planning," *Policy Sciences* 4 (2) (1973): 155–169.

52 Albert W. Dzur, "Trench Democracy in Criminal Justice #1: An Interview with Lauren Abramson," *Boston Review*. Available at http://www.bostonreview.net/blog/albert-w-dzur-trench-democracy-criminal-justice-interview-lauren-abramson.

53 Harry Boyte has been a leader in this movement. See, e.g., *Democracy's Education: Public Work, Citizenship, and the Future of Colleges and Universities*, ed. H. C. Boyte (Nashville, TN: Vanderbilt University Press, 2014).

54 John Dewey, "Education as Politics" (1922), in *John Dewey: The Middle Works, 1899–1924*, vol. 13, ed. J. A. Boydston (Carbondale, IL: Southern Illinois University Press, 1986).

55 Zygmunt Bauman, *Legislators and Interpreters: On Modernity, Post-Modernity and Intellectuals* (Ithaca: Cornell University Press, 1987).

About the Author

Albert W. Dzur is the recipient of the 2017 Brown Democracy Medal. His work in democratic theory focuses on the value of citizen participation in professionalized domains that affect public affairs. He is interested in how collaboration bridges the distance between professionals and communities, encourages mutual trust, develops skills, and builds networks. He is the author of *Democratic Professionalism: Citizen Participation and the Reconstruction of Professional Ethics, Identity, and Practice* (Pennsylvania State University Press, 2008), *Punishment, Participatory Democracy, and the Jury* (Oxford University Press, 2012), and coeditor of *Democratic Theory and Mass Incarceration* (Oxford University Press, 2016). He serves on the editorial boards of *Howard Journal of Crime and Justice* and *Restorative Justice: An International Journal*. He also writes regularly for the *Boston Review*.

Lightning Source UK Ltd.
Milton Keynes UK
UKHW03f0347300318
320269UK00001B/149/P

9 781501 721984